D1366886

HAIL TO MAIL

WRITTEN BY

SAMUEL MARSHAK

HAIL TO MAIL

ILLUSTRATED BY
VLADIMIR RADUNSKY

TRANSLATED FROM THE RUSSIAN BY

RICHARD PEVEAR

HARCOURT BRACE & COMPANY
Orlando   Atlanta   Austin   Boston   San Francisco   Chicago   Dallas   New York
Toronto   London

FIRST CLASS

This edition is published by special arrangement with Henry Holt and Company, Inc.

Grateful acknowledgment is made to Henry Holt and Company, Inc. for permission to reprint *Hail To Mail* by Samuel Marshak, translated by Richard Pevear, illustrated by Vladimir Radunsky. Translation copyright © 1990 by Richard Pevear; illustrations © 1990 by Vladimir Radunsky.

Printed in the United States of America

ISBN 0-15-302164-0

2 3 4 5 6 7 8 9 10   035   97 96 95 94 93

To John Peck

1
Who's that knocking at my door?
His badge is stamped with number 4.
His shoulder bag is big and fat.
His coat is blue—so is his hat.
  Is it him?
  It must be him!
The New York mailman Mister Tim.

  His bag was full
  Of mail today
  From Boston, Austin,
  And L. A.,
  From Reno, Roundup,
  Harpers Ferry,
  Pittsburgh, Plattsburgh,
  Pondicherry.

He started on his rounds at seven.
His bag was lighter by eleven.
He reached the bottom just at three,
Long after he had come to me.

2
"A certified letter for John Peck
Postmarked from Schenectady."
"A certified letter for John Peck?
But he left yesterday!"

"Yesterday? Where did he go?"

"To Boise, Idaho."

3
John Peck is flying
Over wheat fields lying
Like gold across the plain.
The letter follows
Through hills and hollows
In a car of a speeding train.

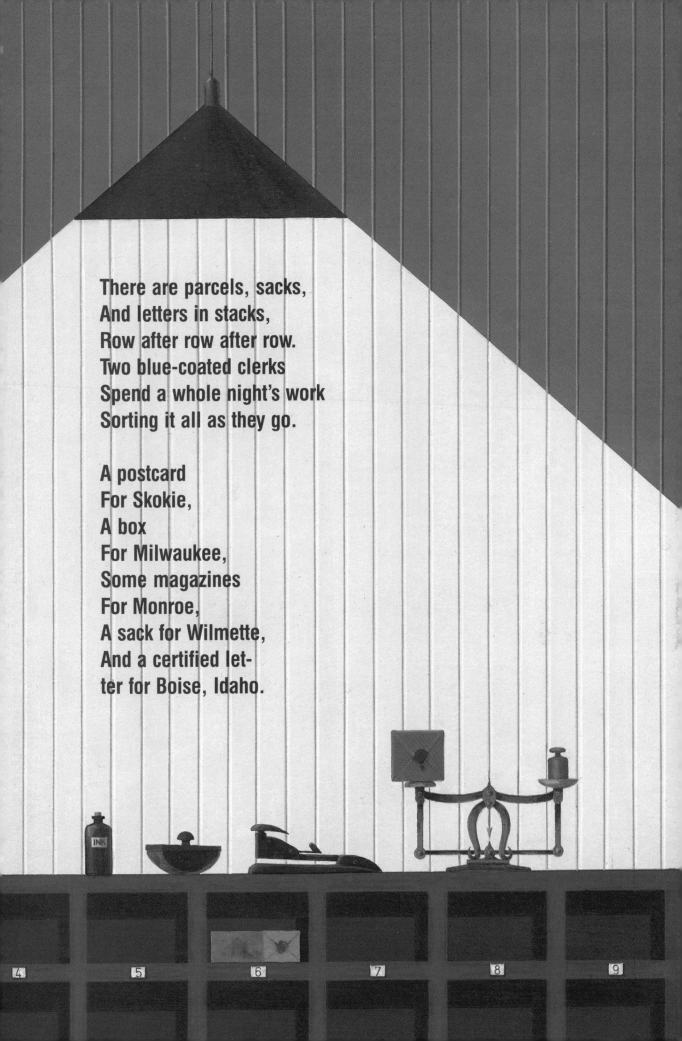

There are parcels, sacks,
And letters in stacks,
Row after row after row.
Two blue-coated clerks
Spend a whole night's work
Sorting it all as they go.

A postcard
For Skokie,
A box
For Milwaukee,
Some magazines
For Monroe,
A sack for Wilmette,
And a certified let-
ter for Boise, Idaho.

4

The Boise mailman strides along.
His bag is heavy, but he is strong.
His uniform might make you laugh
Because it's only there by half—

He has the hat, but not the rest,
Except for the brass badge on his chest.
His step is firm, he's filled with pride,
He holds a letter marked certified.

Around him people hurry by.
Cars honk, trucks roar, babies cry.
Like any other city, Boise
Is always busy and always noisy.

The mailman comes to the hotel.
Of course the doorman knows him well.
"Certified letter for John Peck,
Room 36." "Now, let me check. . . .

Sorry, friend, I hate to say
Peck left for Zurich yesterday."

5
A letter
Had better
Be put in the mail:
By itself it won't get anywhere.
But once it is mailed,
It will roll,
Fly, sail,
Over land, over sea, through the air.

A letter can travel
Without
Any trouble.
Take a stamp
And lick it—
No need for a ticket—
Your passenger's sealed
And ready to whirl
On a few-penny
Journey
All over the world.

And it won't eat or drink
On the way.
And there's only one thing
It will say
As it comes down to land:

6

What a beautiful city! The views!
The lake, with its boats and canoes!
The mountains, and also the valleys!
The buses, or trams, or trolleys!

The conductor stands on one leg
And shouts: "Last stop: Griesernweg!"

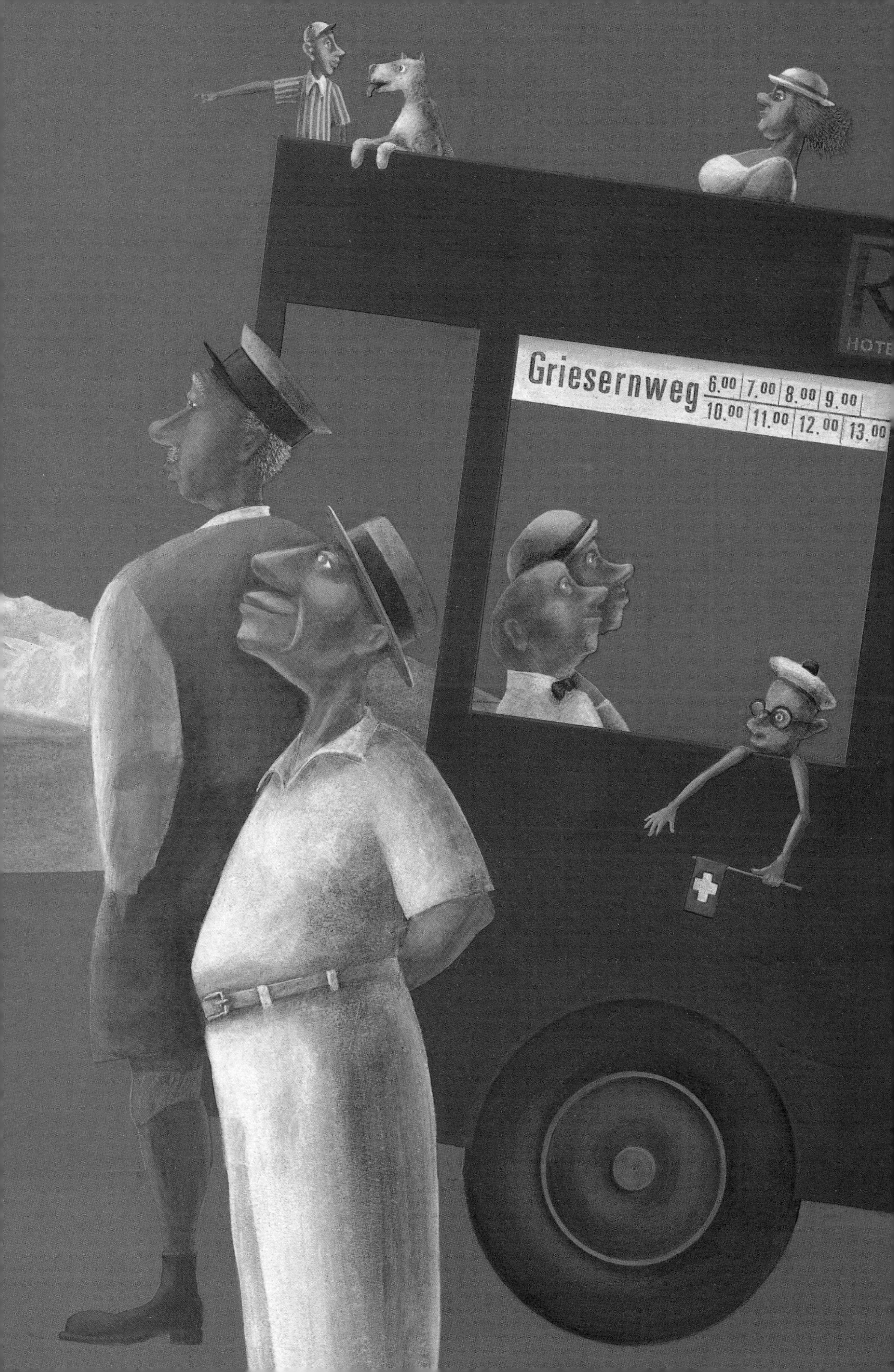

HOTE
Griesernweg
6.00 7.00 8.00 9.00
10.00 11.00 12.00 13.00

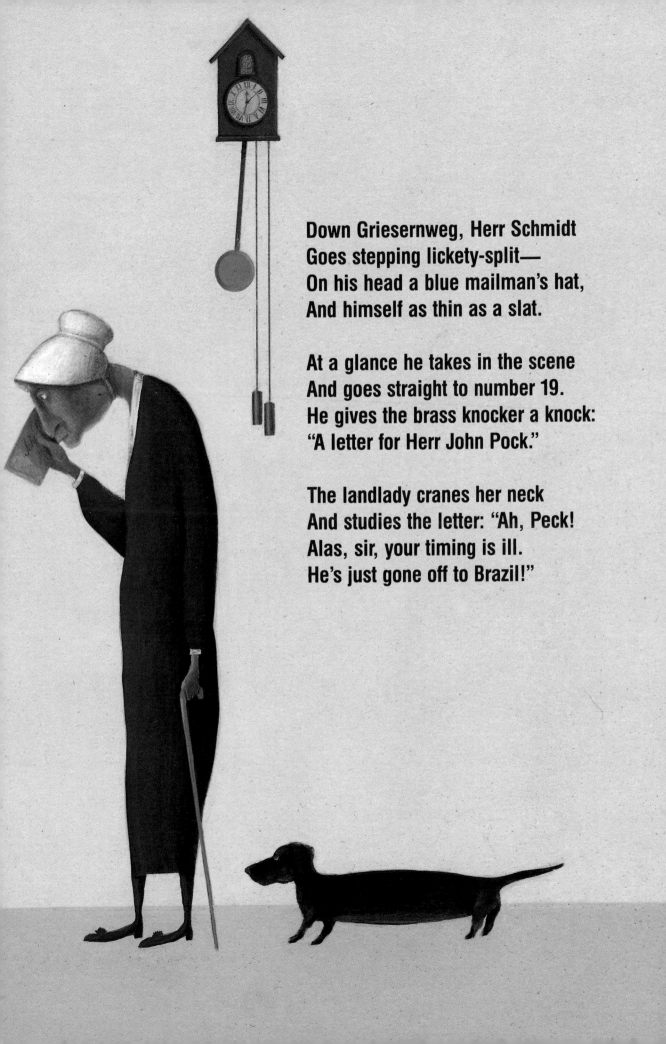

Down Griesernweg, Herr Schmidt
Goes stepping lickety-split—
On his head a blue mailman's hat,
And himself as thin as a slat.

At a glance he takes in the scene
And goes straight to number 19.
He gives the brass knocker a knock:
"A letter for Herr John Pock."

The landlady cranes her neck
And studies the letter: "Ah, Peck!
Alas, sir, your timing is ill.
He's just gone off to Brazil!"

7

The ship will set sail
In less than a minute.
Every cabin is full
Of the suitcases in it.

But one cabin is not,
For there must be a spot
On each ship that sets sail
For the man with the mail.

PIER Nº1

8

The sunset is vermillion.
All weary from the heat,
Bazilio, the Brazilian
Mailman, rests his feet.

A most unusual letter
Is lying in his hands,
Wrinkled, frayed, and tattered,
With stamps from several lands,

And scrawled with a red pencil
Beside the last postmark:
"The addressee has left Brazil.
Please forward to New York."

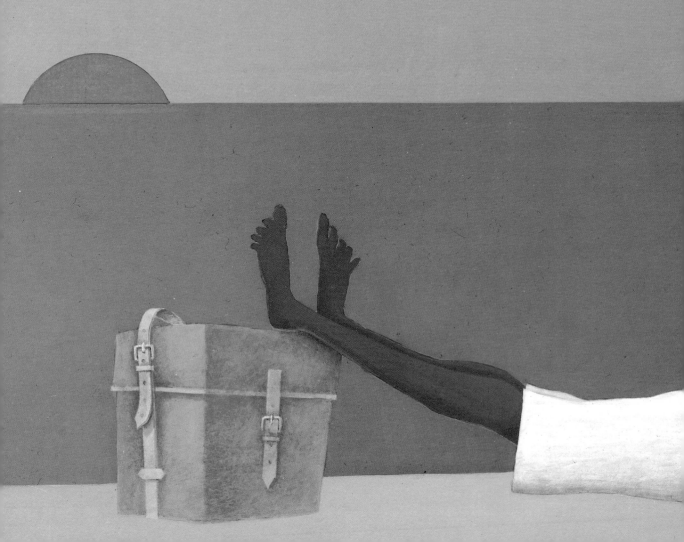

9

Who's that knocking at my door?
His badge is stamped with number 4,
His shoulder bag is big and fat.
His coat is blue—so is his hat.
  Is it him?
  It must be him!
The New York mailman Mister Tim.

I open the door. He hands to me
A certified letter for John P.
  "For Peck? Hey, John,
  Another one!
Or is it the same one? Come and see!"

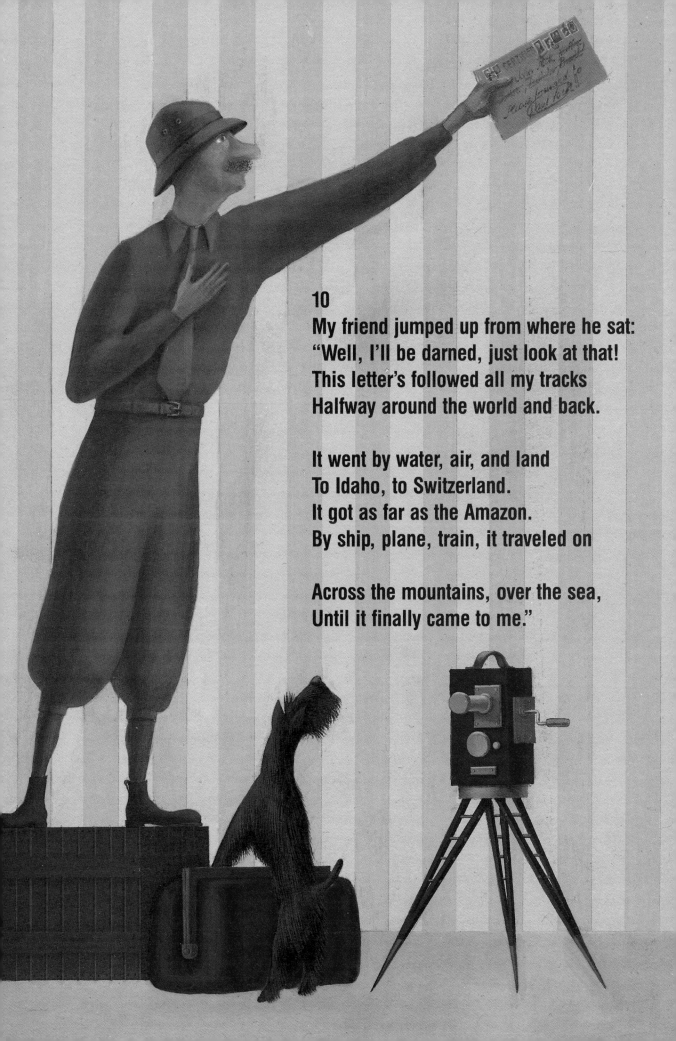

10

My friend jumped up from where he sat:
"Well, I'll be darned, just look at that!
This letter's followed all my tracks
Halfway around the world and back.

It went by water, air, and land
To Idaho, to Switzerland.
It got as far as the Amazon.
By ship, plane, train, it traveled on

Across the mountains, over the sea,
Until it finally came to me."

And all that, thanks to those who go
Through dusty heat and freezing snow—

Glory to them, I say, and hail
To their heavy bags that bring the mail!